Organizing
Your
Kitchen

with SORT and SUCCEED

*Five Simple Steps to Declutter Your
Kitchen and Pantry Shelves, Save Money
& Clean Your Kitchen Countertops*

Darla DeMorrow

Blue
Tudor
Books

Blue Tudor Books www.BlueTudorBooks.com

Published by

Blue
Tudor
Books

BlueTudorBooks.com

Copyright © **2018 Darla DeMorrow**

ISBN 978-0-9833723-5-6 (print)
ISBN 978-0-9833723-6-3 (Kindle ebook)
ISBN 978-0-9833723-7-0 (ebook)
Library of Congress control number: 2018912412

Printed in the United States of America

Information in this book is presented for informational purposes, and is not intended to
constitute professional, legal, financial or other advice. The material may include information,
products or services by third parties. The author and publisher do not assume responsibility
or liability for any third-party material or opinions. Information is provided without warranty,
and readers are advised to do their own due diligence.

CONTENTS

CHAPTER 1

The Heart of the Home

T he kitchen is the heart of a home, or so the saying goes. Even people who don't cook still hang out in the kitchen. Even people who don't hang out in their kitchen store all sorts of important stuff there.

We often want perfection in the kitchen. We see a magazine or social media picture and try to measure up to that (million dollar) photo shoot. But a kitchen isn't a static photo. It's a dynamic place where there is a lot going on. The kitchen is where one of our most basic needs – nourishment – is met. We don't have to be an accomplished chef to enjoy an efficient, attractive space.

You deserve a lovely kitchen.

You can have an organized kitchen that works for you, not against you.

According to a 2018 survey, 81 percent of homeowners report they can't relax if their kitchen is a mess.[i]

By organizing your kitchen for your needs, you can make your entire day go more smoothly. Your organizing efforts may, in fact, contribute to weight loss, fitness goals, better home maintenance, saving money and stronger social connections.

Or you might just enjoy your kitchen more.

You've picked up this book for help with organizing your kitchen. I'm going to give you a system to get it organized, a mindset to keep it organized, and specific tips to address common (and not so common) trouble spots in and around your kitchen.

My sincere hope is that you take this information and do something. Ideally, you'll organize your whole kitchen. Perhaps just clear the countertop. Maybe just organize the pantry. Possibly hire a professional organizer to help you. You can find a Certified Professional Organizer at www.NAPO.net.

Wouldn't it be nice if you didn't have to organize your kitchen yourself? Estimates are that as of 2017, somewhere between 25% and 40% of all U.S. households have some form of home automation, including connected kitchen appliances, thermostats, security, lighting solutions and smart speakers.[ii] Even your robot vacuum counts as a smart home device. Technology is advancing quickly. By 2021, half of all U.S. homes and 36 percent of homes in Europe will have adopted smart technology.[iii] We can imagine a day when your kitchen will organize and clean itself. Sadly, Rosie the robot maid from 1960's animated cartoon, *The Jetsons,* isn't available yet...but she's not far off. Until then, you'll need a system to automate your kitchen the old-fashioned way, and this book is here to guide you.

If you just do something, you probably will have made more organizing progress than you made last week.

If you get started, you'll have an organized kitchen sooner.

Read this short book in about an hour, and then get in there and start organizing your kitchen with SORT and Succeed.

To motivate you even more, I've included three free bonus items, including a checklist, a special report, and a customizable printable. Claim your free kitchen bonuses at Kitchen.HeartWorkOrg.com.

CHAPTER 2:

SORT and Succeed — Review

. . . .

Why re-create the wheel every time you start a new project? People who are overwhelmed at home often feel like they have to figure out how to organize each spot in their home a new way, every time.

People will often spend days, weeks, months and sometimes years working up the nerve and energy to organize a single spot in their home. They are so overwhelmed; they just don't know where to start.

With the SORT and Succeed system, you don't have to re-invent a new approach every time. Just follow the five steps, with built-in obstacle-busters and motivation-enhancers, and you'll have a repeatable process for organizing your kitchen or any space in your home.

In fact, you can apply these same steps to your paperwork, your time, your business and even your money.

You can read more about the SORT and Succeed steps over at www. HeartWorkOrg.com and in the book *Organizing Your Home with SORT and SUCCEED*.

It sounds easy on paper, right? Just do these five simple steps and you'll be organized.

Well yes…and no.

As a full-time professional organizer since 2005, I know that something can be simple and not easy. One of the reasons I wrote this book on organizing is that I know getting organized might not be easy for many reasons. Those reasons include lack of time, lack of focus, emotional barriers, depression, lack of confidence, perceived lack of space, chaotic or missing support systems, lack of aptitude and many others.

According to the study cited earlier, of those surveyed, nearly half think organizing their home is more overwhelming than training for a marathon.[iv]

Here is the good news. Every single person I've ever worked with can get organized. Some need more time. Some need more support. Some need more ideas. Some need changes in their physical environment. But everyone can get as organized as they need to be. The following image shows the SORT and Succeed steps.

1. **S**tart with a written plan
2. **O**rganize into groups
3. **R**educe, release, reset
4. **T**weak
5. **Succeed** and Celebrate

CHAPTER 3

The Difference between Tips and Systems

L et's address a common organization failure before we go too much further, so you can get the most out of this and any other organizing book. Watch out for the difference between tips and systems.

Tips and systems can look very similar, but tips are likely to produce a quick fix that doesn't last. A system, however, is a combination of four parts that facilitate a lasting change:

1. Space
2. Supplies
3. Time
4. A series of steps

The difference between the two might seem subtle, but having systems in your home will produce an organized home. Let me give you some examples.

A tip is to put your keys in the same place every day when you come home.

A system is to install a key hook (supplies) by the door you enter (space) and to build the habit (time) to stop and hang your keys on the hook before you do anything else upon returning home (steps).

A tip is to have your kids do homework every day before bed.

A system is to create a study station (space) stocked with pencils, paper, a calculator, computer chargers and anything else they need to do their homework (supplies), and teach them to use a timer (time) to do their homework immediately after school, and then have you check it and initial it before it goes in the backpack before dinner (steps).

A tip is to clean your fridge weekly.

A system is to wait until the day before you go shopping (time) so there is almost nothing in your fridge (space) so you can quickly wipe down the shelves with white vinegar and a sponge (supplies) and throw out expired food before bringing home new groceries (steps).

If you are naturally an organized person, you are thinking, "Well, of course, the tip listed naturally leads to the system outlined." But that's not universally true.

If you or someone you love has ADHD or any learning differences, or even just a crazy-busy lifestyle, you'll recognize that making the leap from the tip to the system isn't natural for everyone in all cases.

The situations listed above are pretty common, daily situations for most people. However, even organized people might struggle when they encounter a new situation, such as a move to a new house, a diagnosis of an allergy or illness, or a promotion at work. It takes mental energy to go from the situation to the tip to the system. But once you make this leap, systems make daily tasks more automated and less of a struggle.

If you picked up this book for a list of tips, you will be getting so much more.

This book is about creating systems.

If you are a tip junkie, that's cool. But instead of collecting tips indiscriminately, start building the systems that will support your life, your family, your house and your kitchen.

CHAPTER 4

The Difference between Sorting and Organizing

. . . .

You can make a profound change in your home by moving from tips to systems.

You can make another giant leap in your efficiency by going from just sorting your things to actually organizing them, and that's where the SORT and Succeed system comes in.

Sorting is part of organizing, but it isn't the whole story.

Some people have told me that they don't believe a professional organizer can help because they have already sorted everything.

Sorting is just the act of putting things in piles.

Sorting doesn't make you organized.

Take the simple example of a deck of cards. You can easily sort the deck into four different piles, corresponding to the suits: hearts, diamonds, spades and clubs. But if I were to give you a pack of cards to sort at the dining room table, and then you left the room after you sorted them, would you be organized? No. You'd have four sorted piles lying on a dining room table. Your dining room wouldn't be organized. We might still be asking, what should we do with the card piles when we want to eat dinner? Where do the cards get stored in this house? Are there other decks of cards? How can we find them again when we need them?

I worked with a client who initially said to me, "I already sorted everything, so there's probably not much you can do." When I arrived at her home, she did indeed have her papers sorted...all over the living room floor. I couldn't even see the color of the rug, there were so many piles. Several of the piles had tipped and spilled into other piles, so we had to sort them again. And if they had been labeled, which they weren't, they would have had labels like:

Miscellaneous receipts

Random legal stuff

Books I don't know if I need to keep

Stuff my kids probably don't want

Papers I don't know what to do with

Maybe you recognize a bit of yourself in these sorted piles. Do your piles seem organized to you?

Sorting is a good first step. And sometimes it's a good second step, too. You might have to sort your stuff a couple of times before you come to a good decision about what to do with the items, but don't stop at sorting if you really want to become organized.

A big part of what clutters kitchens is paper, and so there is a chapter on paper organizing later in the book. If you need to skip ahead to this section, feel free, but come back here to get through the entire SORT and Succeed system.

Being organized is about being able to find what you need when you need it. Randomly sorted piles on every flat surface don't qualify as an organizing strategy. Yes, there are those who are truly *out of sight, out of mind* people, but that doesn't mean that your whole life has to live in piles at counter-height, out in the open.

Find some organizing systems that work for you and look good, but they have to work first. This is what designers mean when we say *form follows function.* It has to work first, and then it can be attractive. Trying to make something attractive before making it organized and function well for your family just creates clutter out of things that used to be pretty.

So now we know that we are really looking for systems, not tips. And we know that we are going to go beyond just sorting to actually organizing your kitchen. Let's dive into the five steps of SORT and Succeed applied to the kitchen.

CHAPTER 5:

Start with a Written Goal — Step 1

W hat is your goal? Are you trying to get or stay healthy, looking to set a good example for your kids, or are you just tired of fighting clutter in your kitchen?

If you want to get healthy, the kitchen is a great place to start. Research shows that cluttered kitchens prompted people to eat 44% more snack food than a kitchen that was organized and decluttered.[v]

Unless you are working with a paid professional organizer, do not start out with the goal to *organize your entire kitchen*. For most people, it's just too big of a goal to accomplish in the ideal project timeframe of between fifteen minutes and four hours.

Instead, pick smaller goals to organize your kitchen, and tackle them one after the other, perhaps on different days:

Clear the sink

Clear the countertop

Remove or re-organize magnets and notes stuck to the refrigerator door

Baking supplies

Cleaning supplies

Pantry items

Small appliances

Everyday dishes

Grill, picnic and party gear

Refrigerator (inside)

Freezer (inside)

Towels, napkins, placemats and tablecloths

Pick one of these mini-projects, or choose something that's specific to your kitchen, and write down your goal. It can be a single bullet point. It can be on scrap paper or the back of an envelope. Just write down the one thing you are working on today, right now.

Yes, actually writing it down is the first step to getting started. If you've ever gotten distracted while organizing (and really, who hasn't?), then you'll appreciate this. A written reminder can help you stay focused on your project and reel you back into the kitchen when you start to wander off. It's the equivalent of having that professional organizer or good friend there beside you, tapping you on the shoulder, reminding you to stay focused on what you said you were going to do today.

After writing down your goal for this project, actually get started.

Look at your watch right now and plan to get started in about an hour from now, after you've finished this book.

It can be hard to start organizing your kitchen when it all feels too much. It's interesting how a kitchen can feel too small and so overwhelming at the same time. It's easy to go into a downward mental spiral:

I've got to organize the kitchen.

Where do I start?

The dishes are piled up...again.

I loathe doing dishes.

I wish there was a quicker way.

Everybody else seems to be able to keep their kitchen clean.

It would be easier if I had new appliances/fresh paint/more square footage/etc.

I hate cleaning up in here.

I'll never be done.

I'd rather go out for dinner...again!

It doesn't have to be like that. Instead, take just the next right step. Just do the next right thing. I've always found that cranking up the tunes can help organizing go faster. If you can dance it out, you burn calories AND get started. That's a double win. If you would like an audio reminder of what SORT and

Succeed means, <u>there's a jingle for you at https:/heartworkorg.com/sortsong</u>. That's right. I wrote a song for you!

Seriously, you are always going to have a kitchen, whether it's small or large, in an apartment or a house, whether you share it or use it alone. You may as well make peace with your kitchen and find some ways to make it work or you.

So just start.

Just start organizing.

If you aren't sure where to start, start at the door. Pick up the thing closest to the door, and say out loud, "This is a blahblahblah, and I need to do blahblahblah with it." Really, try it. Say it out loud, even if you are the only one in the room. This forces a mental process. It forces you to make a decision about what it is and what needs to be done.

You might say something like, "This is an umbrella, and it needs to go in the mudroom."

"This is a muffin pan, and it needs to get put away with the other muffin pans."

"This is a screwdriver, and it needs to get put away with the tools in the basement."

"This is a box of cereal, and I want to keep all the cereal in the pantry."

The most common problem in cluttered kitchens is the fact that there is no countertop space left. All of the countertop space has been overcome with groceries, paper, dishes and whatever else can be piled there. If that is your situation, the concept of "just starting" is still a roadblock for you, because you have no place to put anything down while you organize.

If your kitchen countertop clutter prevents you from organizing, you probably have stuffed (and over-stuffed) the cabinets, pantry, closets and possibly even the oven. In order to get started, you will need to clear at least a small patch of workspace.

Take a moment to clear off the kitchen table if you have one, along with just a small area on your kitchen countertop, and ideally the sink. You'll need to get to the water at some point to clean up things that you find have spilled or gotten dusty. You just need a small patch of workspace on your table or countertop, about 24" wide, where you can put things down as you group them and evaluate them. It will be tight at first, but by following this system, you'll be able to uncover more and more workspace in a short amount of time. If you are really struggling to find some workspace, make sure that you have a garbage can and some temporary sorting/storage bins available. I go into detail in my book **Organizing Your Home with SORT and Succeed** how to use five laundry bins as sorters with these labels:

Trash

Donate

Recycle

Shred

Elsewhere

The Elsewhere bin is for things you want to keep, but they need to go somewhere else in the house. This one single bin is a very powerful tool. The Elsewhere bin keeps you rooted in the kitchen so you can avoid distractions in other parts of the house while you are working on your kitchen project. If you stay in the kitchen space, there's a much better chance you'll get your project started, and eventually get it finished, too.

See if you are able to clear off most of your countertop by putting dirty dishes in the dishwasher. Maybe you have to empty the dishwasher in order to put dirty dishes in? Take the time now to do that. Quickly throw out trash and expired food. Gather all medicines, vitamins, and first aid items, into another basket or bin, to be organized later.

Here's a tip that will usually get a lot of space for you in short order: Gather all of your papers, receipts and magazines into a single container without look-ing at them. Again a laundry basket or other small bin will work to temporarily contain papers. Now isn't the time to look through piles of paper. Quickly stack them to give you enough space to move. You'll organize papers in a different phase of the project. For now, stacking all of the paper piles together in one safe place will at least create some space to start organizing your kitchen. Stacking papers out of the way will also keep your papers safe from acciden-tally getting dirty, spilled on, or falling into the trash bin.

Doing just these few things will often give you enough countertop space to actually get started.

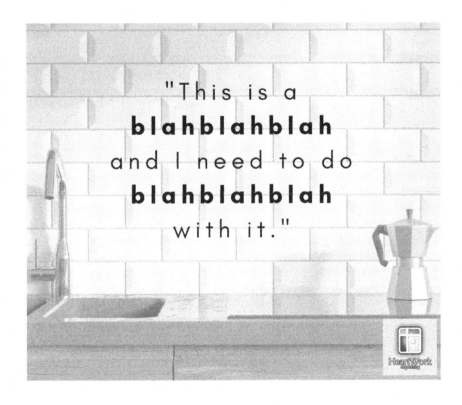

CHAPTER 6:

Organize into Groups — Step 2

Chances are that you already kind of, sort of have items grouped in your kitchen. For example, your silverware (or cutlery or flatware) is mostly in one place. Your dishes that you use every day are mostly in the same cabinets. But some groups have gotten separated, maybe even moved into other rooms or storage areas, such as the basement.

As you start to organize your kitchen things into groups of the same types of things, try to make the groups as large as you can. Too much detail at this stage of the process can really make you crazy. So, a category of *coffee cups* is ideal at this point. Later, you might break that category down further into groups like:

Keepsake mugs that I don't actually use, but feel emotionally tied to

The mugs I use every day

The special travel mugs I like to take in the car

The coffee mugs that came with some dishware, but I don't really use

The Christmas mugs

Etcetera

You can see how a simple category like coffee mugs can get overwhelming if you try to break it down with too much detail early in the organizing process. That's why keeping your groups large and broad makes sense at this point.

Sets of things don't have to stay together just because they came as a set. If you never, ever use the coffee cups that came with your plates, there is no law that says you have to keep the coffee cups until you finally part with the plates, which may be never. Who are you keeping the orphan cups for? Ask yourself why you think you need to keep them. If you are looking for permission to part with a portion of a set, I'm giving it to you now.

Of course, if you have plenty of space, you can keep whatever your heart desires. Organizing doesn't actually require you to toss things from your life. Getting organized is the act of arranging things so you can find them when you need them. You can keep anything, as long as you have space for it.

Organizing kitchen drawers can be fun, especially if you like puzzles. Nobody ever says they have too much drawer space. But almost everyone has lost things in a drawer that is too deep or has too many small items in it.

By going through the drawers, one by one, you will group similar things together and find duplicates, triplicates and more of the same item. If you are on a path to simplicity, you can pick your favorite item and donate the rest.

If you truly have a need for multiple items in the same category, the challenge is then how to arrange or display things in your drawers so that you can always see what you have at a glance, just by opening the drawers.

The simplest way to accomplish this is by using drawer dividers and trays. These can be from a dollar store, or they can be specialty drawer dividers that have features like adjustability. Once you set up your drawers with dividers, label each tray. If you share your space with roommates or family, it's hard to stay organized when they don't know where things go. If you set up systems so people can help you, chances are that they will play along. If you don't set up those systems, not only will they not play along, they might not even realize there's a game being played, so to speak.

I dream of having a kitchen where every utensil is laid out flat in its own space, which is something that you often see in magazine spreads. If that is your goal, then critically assess what you have in your drawers today, and edit down to just the essentials. Eliminate duplicates, things that you never use and things you don't even like. This is where the 80/20 rule is at work. You probably use 20% of what's in your drawers 80% of the time. If you can eliminate the 80% of things that you almost never or absolutely never use, you'll free up valuable kitchen real estate.

I've noticed that people can be very happy with one or two or three of something that they really love, rather than a bunch of the same thing that they don't like at all. You really only use your favorite three pots and pans. You really only use one, two or maybe three of your favorite knives. You are more likely to wash your favorite so you can use it, than allow yourself to use the not-so-nice one at the back of the drawer. You may have nice things, but you always tend to use your favorites. We all do it.

If you aren't certain you can live without that third potato masher, the funky lemon zester and that bunch of gaskets for some appliance that you can't quite recall, then use this strategy that I call *aging out*. Remove all the items that don't make you happy, and put them in a box in a storage area, like a closet. Label that box with today's date, and a note to throw out in one year. Label it in LARGE letters, not small, hard to read handwriting. If you haven't needed to retrieve anything from that box in a year, then you are in the clear to toss or donate those items. If you do need to use a melon baller in a couple of years, you can borrow one from a friend. If you do need to buy it again, it will be money well spent, given that you've enjoyed the added space in your kitchen since you last owned one.

Creating an organized drawer with drawer dividers is a somewhat advanced organizing skill. It takes a bit of trial and error to find an optimal arrangement for the right drawer divider and the right kitchen utensils. Don't try to take on that task just now. We'll come back to that in the T, Tweaking, step of SORT and Succeed. If you try to get the perfect arrangement in your drawers on step two, you are likely to get frustrated and abandon your organizing project altogether. There will be time to make it pretty later, I promise.

If you are looking for a quick organizing project with a big payback, go find where in your home you are storing air.

Empty boxes, plastic bins, shoe boxes, wicker baskets, plastic food storage and glass jars are storing air.

Group these things together out of your workspace while you continue to organize your kitchen. It's kind of satisfying to see the pile of empty containers growing over in the corner while you are organizing your kitchen cabinets. This gives you an idea of where all that space was hiding. Also, in the very next step of SORT and Succeed, you may want to re-use some of those containers when you reset your kitchen.

If you have a large stash of empty containers, you might have thought that the latest bin or box would work out better than some earlier ones...but there was never a good time to look at them all and decide.

Today's the day.

If you've got cabinets full of empty glass jars while food and dishes sit on your countertop, this is an easy fix with just a few minutes of organizing.

If you are tripping over a cluttered pantry while you store containers, paring down your empty box collection will uncover the space you've been missing.

Your organizing containers may be the worst clutter culprit. Do you have empty bins that are storing air, but are meant to help you organize?

Make a decision that you will stop storing air.

CHAPTER 7

Reduce, Release, Reset — Step 3

O nce you have gone through your entire kitchen by organizing into groups, you can then begin step three, which is to reduce, release and reset. Once you have an entire group of things together, you can much more easily make decisions about what fits, what stays and what goes.

Going back to our coffee mug collection example, it's hard to decide if one particular mug should stay or go if you are only looking at one mug. But if you have 50 mugs in front of you, it's very easy to remove the ones that are chipped or stained or shaped oddly or just aren't your style. You can reduce your collection easily when they are all together, because you can quickly compare the merits of each.

Sometimes we let the container do the reducing for us. For example, a shelf can be the container for our mugs. If the shelf only has space for twelve mugs, and I have fifteen mugs, maybe that's a sign that I really need to get it down to twelve mugs.

You might be reading this and think, "But I've tried to reduce the amount of stuff in my kitchen. I just can't do it because I love everything in it. Or I used to love it, and so I might love it again. Or what if I need it someday????"

I promise, once you start pulling items out of cabinets and off shelves, you will find things that you forgot you had, items that you truly don't want once you see them, and you might even find items that have broken, rotted, or been destroyed by pests. When that happens, it's a lot easier to part with them!

You'll be releasing things that fall into a few different categories, including food, paper and others.

REDUCING FOOD

If you find you have more food than you can eat, consider donating it to a local food pantry before it expires. There are food pantries in every corner of the US. Often they are in churches and government offices as well.

If you find a lot of expired food in your pantry, that is a sure sign that you can purchase less food in the future, which saves money in your budget and the space on your shelves. You might have gotten in the habit of filling up the shelves in your pantry or basement when your family was larger. But if you live within a half an hour of retail stores, as most Americans do, there is no reason to keep a pantry stocked with so much food that it goes bad before you can enjoy it.

People think of an extra freezer in the garage as a safe place to put extra food, but there are risks there, too. A power outage can cause a huge loss in frozen food. Also, the freezer itself could be costly to operate. Many people end up with an old refrigerator in the garage when they purchase a new refrigerator for the kitchen, but that's not a wise move. Old refrigerators and freezers can consume as much as four times more energy than newer models and could be costing you up to $150 a year in electricity.[vi]

RELEASING KITCHEN ITEMS

If you are ready to part with dishes, pans, utensils and other kitchen items, batch them and donate them to your local thrift store. Don't spend time trying to find the right, best home for them among your group of friends. That isn't your expertise. Thrift stores, however, are experts in making the right goods available to the right buyers. Donate and move on.

REDUCING PAPER

In chapter 11 we'll talk about where the paper will go in your kitchen, but for now, just decide if you even want paper, books and such items in your kitchen. If not, designate a desk or other space outside of the kitchen for papers. You can skip ahead if paper is your biggest clutter problem.

RELEASING OTHER ITEMS

Hopefully you've noticed what catch-all items have ended up in the kitchen. Shoes, tools and electronics are common things that migrate to the kitchen, but you might find others. As you've been organizing, you might have put these into your Elsewhere bin. If these things have another permanent home, now is the time to take a short break and return them to where they belong. Just a quick trip around the house to drop them off is all you need. Be sure to not get distracted and start organizing another space in your house. Return to the kitchen as soon as possible, within five or ten minutes.

RESETTING THE KITCHEN

Now you are ready to reset. You might be tired. You might be a bit frustrated. But guess what? You are almost done!

As you start to put things back, give yourself permission to try out ideas for better organization.

For example, maybe you've always had the coffee cups in the cabinet to the right of the sink, but your new coffee maker sits to the left of the sink. Does it make sense to move the coffee cups over to the cabinet on the left?

Or maybe your coffee cups have always taken up a whole cabinet, all the way to the top, and you could never reach the ones on the top. Does it make sense to move them to another cabinet where they can all be together on a wider shelf that is easier to reach? Perhaps making that change leaves the top shelf free to store something that you almost never use.

When you reset your kitchen, don't just do what you've always done. Try something new. Make things easier to reach. Store rarely-used items completely out of the kitchen, perhaps in the pantry if you have one, or maybe in the laundry room, garage or basement. Temporarily use shoeboxes or plastic food containers inside a deep drawer to see if dividing up a drawer makes sense for you. Try adding clips or hooks inside doors for smaller items that you reach for all the time. Consider a hanging rail up on the wall or backsplash to get things up off the countertop. All of those cute ideas that you've seen in the magazines and on Pinterest? Now is the time to see if they could really work for you.

This act of resetting takes some time. If you are organizing your kitchen on your own, without help, you will likely need to plan a second day to finish your project. You want to take this on when you aren't rushed. You don't need to buy anything yet, but feel free to start making a shopping list for things that might make your space work even better. If family members have thoughts for the space, let them weigh in now.

Corner cabinets are a challenge, and resetting them is always a little frustrating. In general, we try to place the low-use items back in those dark corners. This is a great place for the huge roasting pan that you use exactly once a year and the appliance that you haven't used lately but aren't quite ready to part with.

If you are unlucky enough to have one or more corner cabinets or even worse, the deep, dark corner cabinet known as a "blind corner," there are ways to make that space more usable. You can retrofit a lazy Susan or a sliding shelf into those awkward spaces. You can add a light. This can be a fairly simple DIY project, or you can hire a handyman. For about $200 or less, you can make those spaces work so much harder for you. Remember to request your free report on **10 Ways to Make Your Corner Cabinets Work Better** at Kitchen.HeartWorkOrg.com.

Organizing your kitchen by going through this entire five-step process is definitely worth the time you'll spend. After all, you are making space to take better care of yourself and your family. Even if your family members all have four paws, everyone will be happier when your kitchen is more organized.

But there are plenty of other benefits to keeping your kitchen organized. Keeping your countertops clear, or at least not using them as an overflow pantry, actually has observable health benefits. A 2015 Cornell study found that what's on your counter might predict your weight.[vii] Women who stored snacks, cereals and sodas on their countertop were on average 20 pounds overweight, compared to women who stored fruit on their countertops and were normal weight.

Does that give you the motivation to keep organizing?

CHAPTER 8:

Tweak — Step 4

. . . .

You can organize your kitchen using what you have right now. But once you've gone through the first three steps of SORT and Succeed, you might want to tweak your space to make it prettier or more efficient. Here are some of my favorite organizing tweaks and supplies to keep your kitchen organized.

SPICES

Spices come up in nearly every discussion about organizing a kitchen. People get very worked up about how to store spices, but the fact is, there is no single best way to store them. The best way for you is a function of your household space, your budget, your style aesthetic, your visual needs and your family's or housemates' needs. In general, there are a few things that you want to avoid. Avoid keeping spices in a warm, sunny spot, as they will deteriorate faster. Avoid keeping them past their expiration date. Avoid buying large quantities that you can't use before they expire. Avoid adopting a storage solution that looks pretty in a magazine, but doesn't really work for you. Finally, avoid the temptation to think all your spices must be displayed in the same size and style containers. You do not need to decant your spices, especially if you don't have them on display. Decanting from the original container into a container that matches your set may look nice, but as a practical matter, it often creates waste and frustration.

Some storage options for spices include:

- Pairing magnetic storage tins with a metal strip bracket mounted to the wall or door.

- Storing quantities of spices you commonly use together in a spice tiffin, which is common in Indian cooking.

- Laying them flat or partially raised (using a tray designed for this purpose) inside a drawer, which allows you to see the jar labels.

- Standing them up inside a deep drawer, and labeling the tops with craft labels, so they are easy to see.

- Placing them on lazy Susans inside a cabinet, which makes it easy to bring the items in the back up to the front with a convenient swivel.

- Adding racks to the back of cabinet doors or closet doors, and lining up jars and tins single file on the racks.

- Adding a pull-out shelf to a cabinet, making the items in the back accessible.

- Creating meal baskets or meal groupings in your pantry, placing spices with foods they are usually combined with. I do this with my go-to breakfast. My cinnamon and vanilla stays with my dry oatmeal in the cabinet, not with the rest of my spices that are grouped together in a drawer.

However you store your spices, make sure they are well-labeled, so you can see and locate what you need, when you need it.

KNIVES

Similar to spices, there are many ways to store and organize knives in the kitchen. However, the most important thing is that you have a selection of knives that you love to work with, and that you keep them sharp. It doesn't matter if you have a large set of knives, or a whole drawer full, if you only use one or two knives each day. That's the 80/20 rule again. To make space, donate knives you don't use, and find a professional in your community who sharpens knives. Take your favorites to be sharpened once a year. A dull knife is actually a hazard in the kitchen.

Some storage options for knives include:

- Using a countertop knife block to store your favorites. If your block has a slant to it, slide the knives in with the flat side on the bottom to keep the blades sharp. Or use one of the newer styles of knife blocks that have flexible rods, instead of pre-cut slots, to hold the knives inside a frame.

- Mounting a magnetic strip on the wall, and hanging knives by magnetic force to their blades.

- Purchasing drawer inserts with knife slot separators. These can be custom or off-the-rack inserts. You'll need a large amount of drawer space for this option.

- Putting knives in a drawer section. This seems to be what most people actually do. To keep them and yourself safe, purchase inexpensive acrylic drawer dividers, and group the knives together by small, medium and large sizes. Always put them away with the handles on the same end, to avoid accidental cuts.

- Protecting yourself and your blade with individual blade sheaths made of plastic or wood. Purchase the right size to protect your blade.

SPECIAL DIETS

Everybody's got some special food concern these days. My own daughter was recently diagnosed with serious nut allergies. I promptly came home and ate or disposed of many items in our pantry. But you don't have to have a diagnosis to change your diet. Perhaps you are one of the millions of people who have gone vegetarian, vegan, paleo, ketogenic, sugar-free, fat-free, gluten-free, low-carb, low-cholesterol, low-salt, kosher or organic. You may have changed your intentions, but did you change your kitchen? Imagine that you are moving into your house for the first time. Give yourself permission to change your kitchen to help you reach your nutrition goals. Would you make your spices easier to get to? Do you want to grow fresh herbs to spice up your diet? Do you want to bake more at home to reduce the sugar in the baked goods your family eats? You may have to move things out of the way that you used to use, and now don't use any longer. For instance, if you no longer eat bread, why is the bread box still on your countertop? If you want your family to eat more fruit, do you need to put fresh choices out on the countertop each morning? Do you want to put your toaster in the pantry and give that spot to your blender so you can make kale smoothies more often? Make sure that the things that you need for your ideal life in the kitchen have a designated place. Don't hang onto that cake-pop baker if you don't eat bread or sweets. Send it on to a new family who may use it more than you did. Don't just have things in your kitchen because they've always been there. Make the right things easy to access, clean and store. That includes dishes, utensils, appliances and food itself.

EASY REACH SNACKS

Make it easier to display healthy snacks on your organized countertop by repurposing a colander or large glass bowl. If you wash fruit before setting it in the bowl, you won't get fruit flies. By putting out nutritious food for anytime snacking, you'll reduce the urge to go looking for less healthy alternatives. Let your family know that anything in the bowl can be eaten by anyone at any time, and let kids serve themselves.

LABEL

Label items in your fridge and freezer with colorful label tape. You can either label the sections where food should go (cheese, lunchmeat, fruit, condiments, etc.), label the containers themselves (meatloaf + date), or both.

RISERS

Pantry step risers should be in every pantry. Most pantry shelves are anywhere from 12-24 inches deep. Once you've placed one can in front of another on a regular shelf, you can't see what's hidden in the back. Step-risers are mini-bleachers for your food. You may need to adjust the height of your pantry shelves to use these effectively, but once you do, you'll have a clear view of each item sitting on each step, and you'll always know what's in the back of the pantry.

LIDS

Lids, lids, and more lids are a common cause of kitchen clutter. You can organize them with a clever, easy to install pull-out lid organizer. You could also use something you probably already have, a long plastic bin that is not too deep and easy enough to slide in and out of your cabinets. I've worked in some households where they prefer to snap lids on before putting containers in the cabinet. This requires a lot of space since you are storing air, but if your kitchen is large enough, it might be a good option for you. If the lids are attached to the bins, you won't lose the lid, but you might need even more space to store your plastic because they take up a larger footprint. Plastic bins with attached lids are usually tipsy because the lid hangs off of one side, so you may find they don't store well on a cabinet shelf. They might store more neatly in a drawer.

BATTERIES

Batteries clutter up the kitchen drawers fast, and who knows if they are fresh or dead? A handy battery organizer can be mounted on the wall to get batteries out of your junk drawer. It has plenty of storage for batteries of different sizes and has a handy built-in tester.

JARS

Use simple mason jars with erasable labels to store long-lasting dry goods in your pantry. You can either buy jars for this purpose or you can re-use mason-style jars that you purchase food in. Some brands of spaghetti sauce, for example, come packaged in a mason jar. Just wash the jar and the lid, remove the label by soaking the jar in warm water, and you have a completely free storage container for dry goods like beans, pasta, small crackers, nuts and dried fruit. The plastic bags that these types of pantry staples often come in are too slippery and disorganized to sit nicely on shelves. Transferring them to see-through jars keeps them fresh, pest-free and more organized on shelves.

CORDS FOR ELECTRONICS AND APPLIANCES

The fix for countertop cords is so easy. Mount a medium sized 3M Command hook on the back of a stand mixer or other appliance. Be sure to mount it high enough to hold the cord, but low enough so it doesn't interfere with the operation of the appliance. Also, only mount 3M Command hooks to appliances that don't get hot, such as a stand mixer or a blender. Don't ever mount them to slow-cookers, rice cookers or other devices that create heat.

Clean the spot you intend to stick. Alcohol works best. The 3M Command hooks come with a double-sided strip that you just peel, peel, and stick. Wind a hook and loop strip (commonly called Velcro) to keep the cord neatly coiled.

Voilà. Cord contained.

A clean countertop, where you don't have to fight with cords, is easier to organize.

I love charging stations because they keep all the gadget cords for electronics and small appliances hidden with an internal power strip, so just one cord gets plugged in. Very smart.

KITCHEN ACCESSORIES

What about those accessories that come with a stand mixer, fancy blender or other appliances? Extra paddles, gaskets, blades and covers seem like they might be useful...if we ever figured out how to use them. The 80/20 rule definitely applies here, since most of us have one or two go-to tools, while the rest of the accessories just get in the way. The one I always use lives on the appliance, and the others live in the cabinets. If an appliance comes with several small parts, gather them together in a small bin to keep them together.

Here's a way to stop them from taking up any shelf space. Apply some medium or large 3M Command Hooks to the inside of a cabinet wall or door. Hang extra appliance accessories from the hooks, easy to reach and up off the shelves. The only tricky part about this is to be sure you aren't mounting on a door where they will bump into an inside shelf or something that you store inside the cabinet. It's easy enough to eyeball.

UNDER SINKS

Sinks are another household hotspot that most people are always trying to tame. Usually, the cabinet under the sink is just one big open space that gets easily disorganized. One of my very favorite organizing tools is a set of drawers made specifically for this space. You can buy stacking under-sink drawers online and in local big box stores in the organization section. Get ones that are heavy duty enough to hold your gear. They should screw down into each other. It's even better if they screw into the cabinet itself. Metal under-cabinet drawers will operate better and last longer than plastic units, but sometimes the plastic units are more adjustable and might fit in your space better. Some have built-in dividers inside the drawers, which make it easy to organize and help keep small items off the countertop.

CLEANING SUPPLIES

Many people stash their cleaning supplies under sink cabinets, despite the danger that cleaning supplies pose to small children and pets. Even if you don't have kids in the house, this can still pose a hazard for grandchildren and visitors. Besides making those big under-sink cabinets easier to use by adding the drawers referenced above, try just reducing the amount of cleaning supplies you buy, store and use (or don't use, as the case may be). When you go through the SORT and Succeed steps, you'll probably find that you have groups of similar cleaners. You'll have two cleaners for the stove top, five countertop sprays, and three dish detergents with just a little left in each bottle. Use them up. Toss the ones you hate. Find one all-purpose cleaner and just use that. Avoid buying new cleaners from the store. Learn how to use just a few kitchen staples, including baking soda, white vinegar, salt and lemon juice, to clean most things. Regular dish soap and hot water is as effective as many chemical sprays, and much less harmful to the environment and your health. There are plenty of good references on green and DIY cleaning solutions. Your kitchen real estate is valuable. Most homes I've organized can free up quite a bit of space by reducing the number of cleaners they keep on hand. Store the remaining few cleaning solutions in a cleaning caddy, and use the space under your kitchen cabinet to store tall baking trays or bulky appliances.

DRAWER DIVIDERS

You have probably already loaded your things back into your kitchen drawers in step three, back when you reset the kitchen, but you might want to take another look at the drawers now. To make the most of your drawers, experiment with both the size of the dividers and the items in them. Entire video game fortunes have been made on spatial optimization. (Who remembers Tetris?) This is where the ability to fiddle and tweak comes in handy. Professional organizers may see the best placement for drawer contents in their mind's eye, but they are also willing to try several combinations before calling it done. In other words, don't get frustrated if something doesn't seem to fit. Treat it like a game.

You can either go with a bunch of small divider trays, arranged in a combination that works best for your drawer, or you can try an adjustable drawer divider, which I find is usually the best option for drawers over 12" wide.

Use the space up front in the drawers for things you use every day. For me, that means the apple slicer, pizza wheel and pie servers are all in the front of the drawer. Many people like to keep the corkscrews and church keys (bottle openers) up front. Do what makes you happy.

Don't make the knives and graters fight with the spatulas and ladles. Someone is going to get hurt.

These small changes can make a huge improvement to one little corner of your world.

KITCHEN UPGRADES

You probably already have everything you need to get organized. But sometimes swapping out an item that you've owned forever for a newer model can make a huge difference. And no, I'm not talking about your coffee maker. Take the example of my whisk upgrade. I don't often use a whisk, but when you really need one, nothing else works quite as well. I owned a whisk for years. Everything fit very nicely in my drawers...except that darned whisk. I was tempted to toss it, but my inner chef prevailed, so I kept it.

Then one day I saw a flat whisk. It folds flat for storage and pops out to a standard whisk shape with just a turn of the handle. You know how some women swoon over shoes? Purses? Jewelry? Apparently for me, all it takes is a flat whisk. I hemmed and hawed over such an extravagant purchase. I mean, I already owned a perfectly good whisk. It just didn't fit in my drawer. I eventually did get the flat whisk, and it makes me happy.

Some selective upgrade in your kitchen might make all the difference. Collapsible funnels and colanders, canisters with a wide mouth instead of a narrow one, pull-out shelves, vertical tray sorters and under-coffee maker pod-holders are all examples of small kitchen upgrades that might have a big return.

LAZY SUSANS

Yes, a lazy Susan is old news, but today's new homes have huge pantries, and so they need bigger gadgets. You might need a larger turntable, as large as 18" diameter, which works perfectly in the corner of a pantry. Or instead of adding one lazy Susan, add three smaller ones in the same space. If you are afraid things will fall off the sides, opt instead for turntables with taller sides. Even a humble turntable has options for different spaces.

COFFEE AND TEA

Tea and coffee take up so much space in kitchens today. Many people devote an entire cabinet or pantry shelf to their favorite brew. Do you know how much air people store in half-empty tea boxes? Instead of leaving a few bags or pods in their boxes, eating up precious kitchen space, consider a coffee pod drawer that fits under your coffee machine. Move individual tea bags out into a container or drawer where you can find all of your teas. You've probably seen a fancy tea box at a hotel or upscale restaurant. Use a small tea box at home to save space and keep beverages more organized. You'll love not having boxes and tins shoved into the cabinets.

SHELF COVERS

There's a low-budget upgrade that solves a common pantry problem for homeowners who just aren't that handy. Cover wire shelves with a liner to make them more attractive and useful. A company called Help My Shelf makes an affordable, specially designed plastic mat and front bib that adds function and a clean look to your pantry in minutes. You can also just cover wire shelves with plastic shelf liner or acrylic sheets cut to size at your local hardware store if all you want to do is cover the wires.

PULL-OUT SHELVES

It's frustrating when you can't get to the back of the cabinet, especially if you have mobility issues. Kitchen organizers I can't live without are pull-out shelves (also called roll-out shelves). With just four screws and about ten minutes to install, you can instantly upgrade your kitchen.

Even if your cabinets are neatly packed, you might not be able to get to everything if you have fixed shelves. Adding pull-out shelves that are sized to your cabinets does eliminate a couple of inches on either side, but it is a good trade for actually being able to get to the stuff at the back of the cabinet.

Making this upgrade is easy. Just measure from left-to-right on the inside of the front frame of the cabinet, or from the inside of the hinges if they extend past the cabinet frame. Order the size that is closest to your size. Be sure to verify the depth and order that correct size, too. You can find pull-out shelves now at big box home improvement stores, organization stores and online.

CHAPTER 9:

Succeed and Celebrate — Step 5

. . . .

Congratulations. You've organized your kitchen, or more likely, some specific part of your kitchen. Choose one of the mini-projects outlined in chapter five, one after the other. It gets easier with each project completed.

It's important to take time to celebrate because it trains your brain how to organize. You want to compartmentalize the job you just did, call it done, and be able to mentally move onto the next project. Without that mental break and celebration, you might feel like you are always organizing, and that's no fun.

There are brain neurochemicals that are released into your bloodstream when you look at something pleasant. If you take a moment to step back and enjoy your organized pantry shelves, it will have a physically positive effect on your brain. Taking a picture and sharing it with your online friends is also a way to signal to your brain that you've completed a project.

Don't we all like the feeling of a job well done? Our kids get a thrill when they hand in an assignment to the teacher and receive it back with high marks. We get a thrill when we pass our driver's test for the first time. Many people participate in 5k races to earn medals and motivation to keep jogging throughout the season.

Who gives you that feedback when you are organizing the kitchen? Probably no one.

That's why I recommend choosing a reward to keep motivating yourself. For some people, the visual peace and finished project might be reward enough. But if that doesn't do it for you, choose any other reward that makes sense. Ideally, your reward would be an experience, rather than more clutter that you have to organize.

Perhaps you've wanted to try a meal-delivery kit.

Perhaps you'd like to update one of your kitchen tools, like my flat whisk in the Reduce, Release, and Reset chapter.

Perhaps you'll be able to schedule the painter for a new paint job, now that your countertops are clear.

There are many, many good rewards you could pick.

Don't skip this step. It's an important one.

CHAPTER 10:

Fridge, Freezer and the Other Freezer

It's hard to hit your kitchen goals if your kitchen is sabotaging you, whether you want to get fit, lose weight or declutter. Your refrigerator and freezer are also part of your kitchen organizing project. Set your kitchen up for success to meet your goals. These are some top reasons to organize your refrigerator and freezer:

Save money by not throwing food away

Avoid buying the same things over and over because you can't find things

Save money by having a well-maintained fridge that will last longer

Avoid possible food loss because of a power outage

Organize your fridge and freezer before you go shopping. Organizing an empty fridge should take about ten minutes, and that's time that you will save once you are in the store. It can help you avoid re-buying things you already have, as well as re-buying things your family never quite gets around to eating. If you put it on autopilot, you never have a very big job on your hands.

Eat all the food. The less that's in the fridge, the less you have to move, toss, clean and organize. Toss anything that's not edible. By the time you go shopping, the refrigerator may not be completely empty, but moving everything over to one shelf and wiping down the shelves is a breeze.

The freezer is where good intentions go to die. Keeping it longer does not make it cheaper.

Many families have different favorite meals during different seasons. For instance, summer is when people switch over to a summer/grilling menu. If you shop at the big box stores, you might need room for that mega box of burgers. I tend to eat completely different food in the winter: more comfort foods and less grilling.

Spend a week or two eating down the pantry. See how creative you can get. While you are at it, you are going to come across things that you just would never eat. Toss them.

You won't starve. I promise. (Just like you won't go naked if you organize your closet.)

Don't have enough in the fridge or freezer for a whole meal? Think tapas, small bites.

Turn off the ice maker and toss the old ice. Wash the bin with hot soapy water, then dry.

Use a large cooler or insulated lunch bags to store food while you clean, to keep the food safe.

Remove all the baskets and wipe underneath.

Wipe down the shelves and clean the veggie bins. I keep a bottle of vinegar and water on hand for this and other household chores. It's safe for the kiddos, so you can delegate this task to younger children. They LUUUUUV squirt bottles!

Wipe down the door bins. This is the grimiest part of my fridge. It's also where the out-of-date items hide.

Wipe down the door seal. While you are at it, check the gasket. Put a dollar bill in between the door and the frame. If it pulls out easily, you might need to replace the gasket.

Get under and behind the refrigerator and freezer to vacuum the coils. The appliance won't have to work as hard, and it will last longer.

Decide what goes back in, and where it goes. Compartmentalize where you can. Use plastic or metal bins, labeled with the category. Label sections and shelves inside the freezer and refrigerator, so other people can help you keep it organized.

Park treats out of the way, so you don't see the ice cream every single time you open the freezer.

Freezer meals are so much more sophisticated than the original TV dinners used to be. Complete freezer entrees are often as healthy as they are tasty. Having a few freezer meals on hand is a must for busy families.

Go grocery shopping, and restock a shiny, clean fridge...with no lurking mystery meat or golden oldie leftovers.

Feeling like you can go the extra mile? Make it cute. Use colorful labels to organize inside your refrigerator and freezer so everybody can find what they need.

Does this sound like a big job? It can take longer to write out instructions on how to clean your refrigerator than it does to actually do the job.

CHAPTER 11:

Paper Management in the Kitchen

· ·

A
ccording to a study conducted by Moen in 2015, the biggest pain point is the lack of countertop space while mail clutter takes up valuable kitchen real estate.[viii] But you probably already knew that from your own experience.

Even those who have a home office are often plagued by a universal truth: papers usually come through or get caught in the kitchen. Everyone has good intentions of getting papers over to the home office or kitchen desk, but papers always seem to end up on the countertops again. It is 1,000 percent easier to change your environment than it is to change your habits, so you might just need to let your papers have a home in the kitchen, after all. I'd love to show you where the filing space is hiding in your kitchen.

If you had a safe spot to actually file in your kitchen, you could probably keep the countertops clear for food prep, right? Then meal prep wouldn't be such a hassle. You might enjoy it more, everyone in your family would pitch in, and all the picky eaters would suddenly love what you cook. One can dream, anyway. But first, we have to get those papers off your kitchen countertop. If we're lucky, there's going to be at least one drawer that we can repurpose as a file drawer.

To do this, you need a file frame that is sized correctly for your drawer and can be mounted inside the drawer with just a few screws. As long as your kitchen drawer is more than 10 high on the inside, you'll probably be able to use this. You won't believe how much organizing bang for your buck you'll get from a simple file frame, priced at around twenty dollars.

When properly fitted, a file frame will be as sturdy as any file cabinet. Depending on the frame, you install it with just a screwdriver or no tools at all. If you don't have a kitchen drawer that can be converted into a file drawer, you can purchase an attractive file tote to leave on the countertop. The important features in a kitchen file tote are:

Large enough to hold standard files

Sturdy construction, with metal hanging rails on the top edge

Handles, so you can carry it to where you like to sit to pay bills

Attractive enough to leave out in plain view

In a perfect world, there would be no paperwork at all in a kitchen, but until that day comes, there is one kitchen gadget that you can use to corral bills in a kitchen: the upright napkin holder. A simple acrylic or metal U-shaped upright napkin holder can be the perfect parking spot for bills. The napkin holder keeps important bills and their envelopes together and contained to a small footprint in the kitchen. It keeps the bills standing upright, so they are less likely to get lost under a pile. It is affordable and may be something you already own.

There are many other organizing gadgets and memo boards designed to help with paper management in the kitchen. However, my best advice is to try to get paper out of your kitchen altogether. Add reminders directly to your electronic calendar. Move coupons out to your car so they are where you need them to be. Display art by hanging it instead of piling it. Be ruthless. If you need more help with paper management, how to set up files, and what to do with photos, go to www.HeartWorkOrg.com for more paper articles and classes.

AVOID STACKING PAPERS

in the kitchen

CHAPTER 12

Pantry

. . . .

My definition of organized is: being able to find what you need, when you need it. That is never more true than when you are cooking. A well-stocked pantry is a key to a well-organized kitchen. Your pantry might be a small room off the kitchen, a tiny closet or a single cabinet. My British friends sometimes call it a larder. Whatever you call it, make it work for you.

Remember we talked about tips versus systems and sorting versus organizing? Systems help you keep the pantry organized with little-to-no effort. If you feel like to you have to re-organize your pantry every week, you probably don't really have systems in place.

Work quickly, one shelf at a time, from left to right, to make quick work of a pantry organizing project.

Purge now so you don't get sick later. You may not be able to get to a magazine-worthy pantry in a few minutes, but you can dispose of all outdated and expired food items in about that time. If food doesn't have a sell-by or use-by date, it's too old to take a chance on and should be tossed.

Many people start each New Year with a goal to eat better or get healthy, but they don't really do anything about it. You don't have to wait until the start of the year to get your food organized. If you can find the good snacks, you are more likely to eat them. If you don't buy unhealthy foods, you can't eat them.

Make good choices in the store, and those good choices will follow you home to an organized pantry.

PANTRY GADGETS

Make sure it's easy to see items in your pantry. Use step risers, clear bins that are labeled, and ensure there is good lighting in the pantry to help keep it organized. If you can't see in your pantry, hire an electrician. The money you save from not throwing out stale mystery foods will easily pay for the electrician's time.

The pantry often stores non-food items, too, like lightbulbs, cleaning supplies and infrequently-used appliances. The single most important thing you can do to keep these organized in a pantry is to batch them together in their own bin. Use a large label to clearly mark the contents. Don't make people guess where the lightbulbs went, or your family members might just buy more instead of using what you have.

Use lazy Susans to make full use of corners or high shelves.

If you have adjustable shelves, now is the time to adjust them. Cereal boxes need a taller shelf. Canned goods need a shorter shelf. Adjusting shelves will take a bit of time, but you only have to do it once. Put that extra few inches in the right place.

Keep a small shopping bag on a shelf for dead batteries, so they can be recycled later.

Don't buy anything until after you've already organized and re-used containers that you already own. Re-use mason jars to store dry goods. Former Easter baskets can hold snacks. Clear containers work great in a pantry, but you can also wrap cardboard boxes with paper to stylishly store smaller things like spice packets and coffee pods.

Store paper muffin cups in a tall, acrylic spaghetti holder. It saves space, keeps them neatly contained and you can see what you have.

Display straws in a short flower vase. It makes them easy to grab and makes the pantry prettier.

Most people store their bag clips in a drawer, but why not just clip them on the top of a basket, right next to the chips? It saves you from having to leave the pantry to look for a clip. You can also install a metal strip inside the door and use chip clips with a magnet built-in.

Add a hanging under-shelf basket to an installed shelf to make better use of vertical space.

Add a door-mounted rack to hold snacks and small items that get unruly on shelves.

PANTRY FOOD

It's fashionable but not always practical to shop local and often for vegetables, fruits and grains. Here's how to outfit your pantry so you can always have nutritious basics or entire meals on hand.

Sort food items together. Soups with soups. Baking goods together. Beverages all in one place. You can sort on the kitchen countertop, where you can see how much space you need for each category, and then reset the groups back into the pantry.

Stop buying items you never actually eat, regardless of their health claims.

Keep whole wheat pasta and brown rice on hand for a quick and healthy side dish for any type of meal. Couscous and polenta are also easy-to-prepare staples that fulfill the grain wedge of the plate. You might have grown up learning about nutrition from the food pyramid. If you haven't seen the USDA food guidelines graphic lately, it looks like this:

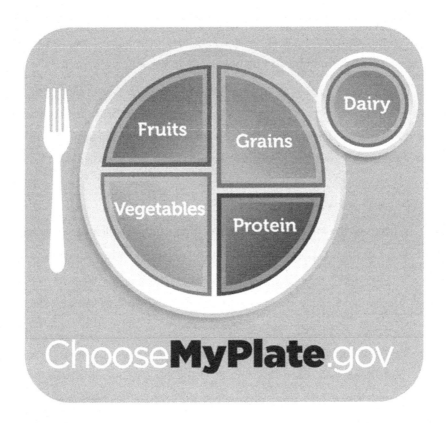

Canned beans are a great way to introduce vegetable-based protein into your diet. Canned meats can be an economical source of protein, especially in soups and casseroles.

Get everything you can except large, heavy beverages off the floor. Storing food up off the floor makes it harder for pests to find. It makes it easier to clean up spills. It ensures that you won't step on things. And it makes it less likely you'll lose things under piles. The floor is not a container.

Heavy appliances and pans need to go at waist level or below. Heavy items like beverages and heavy appliances can be stored on the floor for safety, but I prefer shelves that have been properly reinforced. Heavy items can cause built-in shelves to bow or pull away from the wall over time.

Ideally, anything stored on the floor should have wheels. Use a cart or a platform for sodas or other bulk items. If they have wheels, you'll be able to get to things more easily, and you'll be able to clean better.

Ensure frequently used items are on the easy-to-reach shelves and cubbies. This is where you might need to fiddle and tweak a bit more. Reset shelves. Move things around. Make the space user-friendly. Get the frequently used items out of the back corner and put them front and center in clear containers.

PANTRY MAINTENANCE

When it comes to keeping your pantry organized, keep things simple.

Avoid storing non-food items, like cleaners and lightbulbs, in the pantry. If you must, group them together in containers and assign them their own shelf. These items easily become clutter. You really want to see your foods clearly so you can prepare them easily.

Store food together in a pantry or in cabinets that are close to the food prep area. Keep similar items together. By doing this, you are more likely to use items before they expire. You'll also be less likely to overbuy the same items at the store.

When putting groceries away, put new items behind older items. Use the FIFO (first in, first out) rule.

If you want other people to help in the kitchen, label shelves so others know where items should go.

Follow the 2x2 rule. Don't stack anything more than two items high, and no more than two items deep, unless you are using step-risers.

"Face" your items. "Facing" your canned goods, or turning labels towards the front, instantly makes things look organized. Just rotate the labels front and center, as they would be in a grocery store.

Eat through your food inventory. Eat down to the shelves twice a year. Do the same with the freezer. See how creative you can be with your combinations. I have the luxury of making a game of it, but it's how many people live. When was the last time your kid said, "There's nothing to eat in here?" Show them what that really looks like by emptying the shelves. Most families are surprised at how much food you still have in the house, even when it feels like you have none. When the shelves are bare, it's time to wipe them down, donate your least favorite items (that are always on the back shelves) to the local food bank, and make your shopping list.

CHAPTER 13:

Meal Planning

. . . .

Many people think that meal planning is the worst household chore of them all. If you are the one who usually plans and cooks dinner, chances are that you've had at least a few days when you just feel burned out. #Understatement?

Do you have to feed the kids again today? Didn't they just eat yesterday???

There are several steps to meal planning, and just like you suspected, if your kitchen is more organized, meal planning is easier. If your kitchen is disorganized, meal planning is harder. Good meal planning includes:

Inventory management

Choosing recipes for the next several days

Shopping for ingredients

Prepping and cooking meals

Cleaning up and restocking the kitchen

MANAGING INVENTORY

Learn how to build meals with staple foods. Many staple foods don't expire, or they only go bad after a very long time. Beans, grains, quinoa, dried fruit, honey, whole kernel popcorn and winter squash are some great pantry staples. For more ideas, look back on chapter 12.

CHOOSING RECIPES

Have a meal plan, even if it's a loose one. You need 5-7 meats, 5-7 vegetables, and 5-7 carb dishes in order to have a week's worth of meals for the family.

Plan to have leftovers or takeout one or two nights per week.

Make it easy on yourself. Find 10-20 favorite family meals and rotate through them. No one ever said you have to create elaborate meals, and there's a chance that your people might not eat them if you planned them. Stick with the favorites, and ensure they are well-balanced with good nutrition using protein, vegetables and whole grains.

Once you've chosen your recipes for this shopping trip, write a grocery list based on your meal plan. Even better, write your grocery list in the order that the aisles run in your favorite store. With a little organization at home, you'll save time and avoid having to retrace your steps looking for forgotten items at the store.

Create a grocery list template that you can copy and use over and over again, reducing planning time. Or start by using the list from an online grocery delivery service, even if you are doing your own shopping.

SHOPPING FOR INGREDIENTS

Don't shop hungry. Always eat before grocery shopping.

Have a list, have a list, have a list. People waste both time and money when they buy on impulse. Have a list of the basics that you almost always need, and then add to it.

This is where online shopping works really well. If you have a list of staples that you love to have on hand, those items are perfect for online delivery. Whether you use an online delivery service like Amazon Pantry, or a local service like Instacart or Peapod, you can put those items on auto-delivery so you'll always have the basics on hand.

If you have health goals, or just want to get out of the store faster, stick to shopping the perimeter of the grocery store, where you'll find the fruits, vegetables and fresh foods. Don't wander up and down each aisle...just in case. Head down aisles to find the items on your list, almost with blinders on, in order to get out quickly.

Although warehouse shopping is popular, it also takes a lot of time to cover a large store footprint and is actually designed to entice you to buy more and spend more. Simplify by doing grocery shopping at smaller stores. We just don't need 28 different choices of peanut butter. People are tired when they get home, and adding more decisions to their day can lead to analysis paralysis, where it takes longer to come to a good decision because they are trying to make the perfect decision. When it comes to grocery stores, bigger isn't always better. Trader Joe's, Aldi, even the grocery section of Target stores are better for reducing the feeling of overwhelm found at larger grocery stores. A farmer's market is also generally smaller and might have fresher produce than the stuff in the big stores, although that's not a guarantee.

Load up on fresh vegetables and fruits to have about a week's worth of fresh items on hand. Plan meals to eat the more perishable vegetables soon after shopping. Buy vegetables that are hardy, including root vegetables that can stick around for a few weeks (carrots, winter squash, potatoes, onions and sweet potatoes). Keep frozen fruit and cut vegetables in your kitchen freezer to eat after the perishable produce is gone.

Consider using the cash envelope system to help you cut down on impulse purchases when food shopping. This can save both space and money. Here's how the cash envelope system works: Decide what the right amount is per week or month. Pull that cash out of your paycheck and carry the cash in an envelope marked *Groceries*. As an example, perhaps you decide that $100/week should be enough, then actually shop with that. When you get to the end of the cash in the envelope, you stop spending and get really creative with what's in the freezer and pantry.

Your brain actually acts differently when it is shopping with cash, versus when it is shopping with plastic. Credit cards and debit cards tend to both have the same effect on the neurosystems. We tend to spend at least 20 percent more when we shop with plastic, and some people spend a lot more than that. The science backs up the fact that just shopping with cash can change our habits, so you can look at it as brain training rather than deprivation.

Also, to avoid deprivation backlash, pad your budget number just a bit. So instead of the $100 budget, give yourself a little cushion and call it $120, for example.

Above all, avoid the *what the hell effect* (that's a research term[ix]), which is where you go over budget a little and say to yourself, "What the hell, I'm already over budget, so I may as well not think about it now. I'll splurge now and try again next month." Every tweak to your plan is a chance to adjust, not a punishment or proof of failure.

It seems positively old-fashioned now to shop for groceries with cash. If you have to use plastic, you can establish a modified envelope system with a debit account that you only use for food shopping. Transfer your budgeted grocery money into that debit account regularly, and ONLY use that card for groceries.

After you've paid for groceries, they need to be bagged. If you really want to be efficient at the store, pack your own groceries into groups of products based on where they'll be unpacked at home. In the store, pack bags for refrigerator items, freezer items and pantry items. By packing bags like this, the cold items stay cold, and you save time unpacking. Some of the kitchens in today's homes are huge, so saving steps is a really big deal.

Lastly, and this is not to be overlooked, delegate putting away the groceries once you get home. Kids as young as six years old can help put groceries away. If you label the shelves, your people will know where things go, which makes your job easier. It also trains the kids to help out, and they get a glimpse of what is in the pantry, so they know what is available for dinner or snacks.

PREPPING AND COOKING MEALS

Your family might never be on the same page about what makes a great dinner. Every household should have a few simple meals in reserve at all times that please most people. Dinner doesn't have to be complex, and it doesn't have to be from a powder/box/bag/takeout menu. If you are looking to eat more plant-based/healthy/economical/simple foods, don't overthink it. You don't need the latest trendy food. You don't need meat in every dish. You don't have to go organic. And you don't have to be terribly organized if you can get your meals down to a humble equation...

Vegetables + Protein + Carbs = Dinner

Mac and cheese from scratch is one of my simple meals. Three ingredients. No recipe needed. Boil water, cook and drain the pasta. Add shredded cheese and a can of evaporated milk. Stir. It's hearty enough to pass for a whole meal for one night. Add frozen peas while boiling the pasta to get your greens in. Simple. Filling. Makes enough for lunch the next day.

Keep frozen bagged vegetables (peas, corn, broccoli), side dishes (prepared couscous mixes, mozzarella sticks) and entrees (frozen chicken breasts, hamburger patties, fish filets, pasta dishes, pizza) on hand for easy prep. Family-style portions of lasagna can be kept in the freezer for a few weeks. All-in-one-pan freezer meals like pasta, shrimp and frozen vegetable mixtures cook quickly and look fancy, with no prep work.

Leftovers don't have to look like leftovers. Mix it up a dozen different ways. Combine whatever is in the refrigerator crisper drawer + whatever meat is left over from yesterday's dinner + whatever box of rice/pasta/lentils/grains from the pantry cooks the fastest.

CLEANING UP AND RESTOCKING THE KITCHEN

If you are the only one doing all of these meal prep steps, you are probably exhausted by the time you get to clean up. It is completely ok to ask for help. Don't be a martyr.

If there are more than two people in your house, there is a very simple tip that will help keep your kitchen in top running order. Fill and run your dishwasher every night, and put the clean dishes away every morning.

I used to think that you should only run the dishwasher when it was absolutely, positively full. However, I've learned over the years that the peace that results from always having clean forks far outweighs the possible downside of having one empty slot in the dishwasher load. If you have children living at home, even if they are adults (especially if they are adults?), they can take over the task of putting the dishes away every morning. If you are having trouble staying on top of dirty dishes, leverage the cleaning power of your dishwasher. It costs about $0.28 (US) in electricity and hot water to wash a load, and your sanity is certainly worth that.[x]

If you want to maximize each load, fill it with other things that can benefit from a run through the dishwasher:

Plastic toys

Toothbrushes

Kitchen sponges

Flip-flop shoes

Hand broom and dustpan

Exhaust fan filters. Most people don't even know these are in the bottom of your wall-mounted microwave or stove hood, but these steel filters just above your stove get greasy over time. Pop them in the dishwasher to clean. Lay to dry overnight before replacing in your appliance.

Hairbrushes and combs

Car parts, including removable cup holders and console liners

Pet dishes

Pet toys

Cleanup is where your organizing system might break down. If things get put away in the so-called wrong spots, you might feel like all of your organizing efforts are wasted.

There are two surprisingly easy solutions for staying organized. One is to tell other people in your family, including your spouse, kids, grandma, nanny, and whoever else helps you, where things go. You might have to do this more than once. You might decide you have other battles to fight. You can do this nicely, without attitude or judgment. But if you never tell them where things go, how will they know???

Your organizing systems aren't obvious to others.

You know that *Men are from Mars, Women are from Venus* thing? It turns up in the kitchen, too. He assumes things work one way; she believes they work another way. You can't just put something on a shelf and expect that other people know that it should *always* go on a shelf, or on *THAT* shelf, or *with* those other things sitting next to it.

The other solution for staying organized is to label the heck out of things. This works not only if you live with others, but even if you live alone. If you decide that bowls go on THIS shelf today, then label it that way. You may decide later to make a change, but as long as that label is there, it will be a prompt for you and others.

Seriously, many an organizing client has said to me in an exasperated voice, "My spouse never puts the dishes where I want them." When I point out that I might not be able to put things away for them correctly either, they start to understand the importance of labeling.

When I was first married, I complained to a friend that my husband put away the vacuum cleaner the wrong way. She skipped a beat, gave me the side-eye, and said, "Your husband vacuums???? Maybe you should just be happy he does it at all."

One more thing about labeling: Make the labels large and easy to read. My organizing company has started using only one-inch label tape because it is easy to see. In dim spaces or for people who have compromised vision or limited attention spans, larger labels are definitely better.

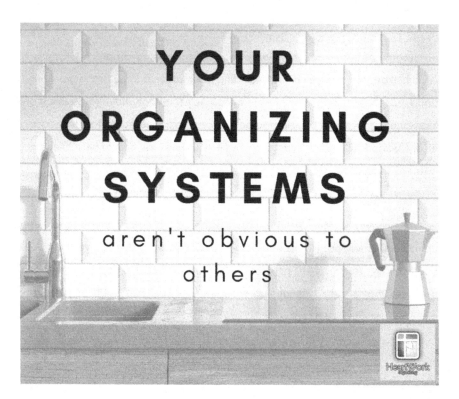

MEAL PLANNING SHORTCUTS

Smoothie Meals

Here's my basic smoothie recipe:

A handful of frozen berries, whatever makes you happy

Two scoops of plain Greek yogurt (a scoop is what you make it)

1 tablespoon-ish of vanilla protein powder

Enough water to cover it all and...are you ready for this?

1/4 of an avocado

When I first heard about putting avocados in a smoothie, my reaction was to make a yucky face. We generally don't think of eating green things for breakfast in our culture. But the avocado is really what makes the smoothie extra creamy, very healthy (so they tell me), and I swear to you I cannot taste it at all.

Also, all of these ingredients are very storable and swappable. You can shop once a week, or even less often, and still have a healthy breakfast or snack at the ready. Buy frozen berries in the big bag if you like smoothies. Swap the avocado for a banana every now and then. Skip the protein powder altogether if you are out, or throw in a tablespoon of peanut butter. Just about any kind of yogurt will work. Mix it up; it's your smoothie. But with a protein boost like this, you are much more likely to stay on track with your fitness goals...at least until noon.

Meals from Your Stand Mixer

Use that stand mixer gathering dust in the corner or, worse, taking up valuable cabinet space, to make more than just cookie dough. Try these tips to make meals using a KitchenAid stand mixer.

Shred chicken by throwing hot-cooked chicken breasts in the stand mixer for 30-60 seconds. Use in your favorite recipe, like tacos.

Egg salad. Use the blade to chop hard boiled eggs. Mix with relish and mustard.

Mashed potatoes. Cook potatoes for 6 hours on low in the slow cooker, first.

Meatloaf can be easily mixed, and goes great with the mashed potatoes.

Pancakes. For sure, you'll make them more often when the mixer is already on the countertop. And yes, pancakes can absolutely be dinner.

Pizza dough. Just add sauce, cheese and fresh toppings.

No-bake pies. You can skip the baking altogether and use a graham cracker crust.

Banana dessert. Mash 3 ripe bananas with a fork. Add sugar to whipping cream using the stand mixer, and blend until you get whipped cream topping. Fold the two mixtures into each other and freeze until solid.

Crust-less spinach and kale quiche (good for breakfast, lunch or dinner)

Herbed Whipped Squash side dish. Just add butter and fall spices.

Chicken and Mushroom Casserole

Black Bean Frittata

Crabmeat Dip (Good for a quick party appetizer.)

Pulled pork. Cook pork shoulder in slow-cooker. When fully cooked but still warm, place chunks of pork in the KitchenAid bowl with a flat beater. Add BBQ sauce on low speed for twenty seconds.

And yes, if you must bake, find a pie pastry recipe to get you started. 'Cause I'm all about the pies.

You can do a quick internet search to find recipes like these. Recipes usually don't require any modification when you are using a stand mixer.

Pulled Chicken Shortcut Meals

You'll want to keep your slow cooker on the countertop when you learn about this dinner solution that works all year long. This dinner tip can become your dinner system. Even without knowing what dinner is going to be, you can start cooking chicken in your trusty slow cooker before you leave the house in the morning. Throw frozen chicken breasts in the slow cooker with a quarter cup of water or wine, add spices if desired, then cook on low for 6-8 hours.

Use any cut of chicken you prefer. They are economical to buy and easy to store. They are a better alternative to those rotisserie chickens from the grocery store because they are so moist in the slow-cooker. This dinner tip works especially well in the summer because the slow cooker doesn't heat up the whole kitchen as the oven does. Even better, it will smell like dinnertime just when everyone is hungry.

Once the chicken is cooked, you have so many options. You can easily shred the chicken with just a fork. It's perfect for so many recipes. Here are ten things you can make later today with slow cooker chicken:

1. Chicken with baked potatoes (Start with the obvious, shall we?)

2. Chicken tacos

3. Chicken salad sandwiches

4. Quick chicken parmesan. Smother in spaghetti sauce and mozzarella, then warm in the microwave.

5. Chicken sloppy joes. Just add your favorite BBQ sauce.

6. Taco salad topped with chicken

7. Mini chicken pizza. Top English muffins with spaghetti sauce, cheese and chicken.

8. Loaded nachos

9. Pasta salad. Pick your favorite combo of pasta and fresh vegetables, add chopped chicken, and cover in Italian salad dressing.

10. Mini chicken and avocado sandwiches on Hawaiian sweet rolls with red pepper hummus spread

Cooked chicken will store for about five days in the fridge, if you don't gobble it up first.

If you are trying to wean your kids off of breaded nugget chicken, try these recipes. Don't be afraid to let them get messy while they are exploring new flavors and textures. It looks like fork food to us, but let them use their hands, and they'll be more likely to try it.

CHAPTER 14:

Recipe Organizing For Family Favorites

. . . .

Y ou are going to love how pretty your recipes are once they are organized. If you are like other people, you might have a little index card box that's stuffed so full it's hard to find anything, a folder with recipes falling out of it, and a stack of cookbooks with just a handful of recipes that you actually use.

What's worse, most of those collections have multiples of the same recipes. There can be so many that it makes it hard to find the favorite, special recipe that you are searching for. Many people pull recipes out from magazines, so they end up with pages with ragged edges and more yummy possibilities than they could ever use.

These days, a smartphone app does a better job of calling up recipes from Pinterest, other cooking apps or our own private cloud storage. But it's tricky to save a recipe electronically and find it again later. And those little index cards where we all kept our recipes thirty years ago? Well, most of us just print out full sized pages from our printers these days, and full-sized recipes don't fit in the index card box. Here's the fix for all of that recipe clutter. Create your own Family Favorites recipe binder.

Supplies:

1. A 1.5" or 2" binder. One with an inside flap pocket to temporarily hold new recipes is ideal.

2. One pack of plastic page protectors. I start with a pack of 200.

3. Two packs of pretty section dividers

4. Scissors

First, sort recipes into categories and remove duplicates. Because this is your binder, you can create the categories that you actually use, not arbitrary categories from a recipe box. Many ready-made recipe organizers group soups and salads together in one section. But in my world, those are two different and distinct categories, so they are in different sections in my binder. If you are a vegetarian, you might need a section for beans and lentils. I've always kept my favorite slow-cooker recipes in their own section. I also added a section at the back for green cleaning recipes that use things like vinegar and lemon juice, things you mostly find in the kitchen. I never had a good place to store them, but now I do.

A pretty little table of contents will help identify which section to head to.

Trim the ragged edges off magazine pages, if needed. Slide recipes into page protectors. Page protectors keep the recipes cleaner in the kitchen.

Reassemble your favorite recipes into the binder by section. The binder format makes it easy to try a recipe, then rotate it to the back of the section if you want to keep it, or remove it altogether if you don't. Try the recipes as they rotate up to the front of the section. Use the binder as a shortcut for meal planning, as you work your way through your recipe binder.

The last step is to add a pretty Family Favorites recipe binder cover. This is the really important part, so your family will know where the family secrets are kept. I've added a free printable recipe binder cover, spine, and table of contents as a bonus for you. Download the Family Favorites binder cover and 2 more bonuses to keep kitchens organized at http://kitchen.heartworkorg.com.

You can also download a customizable version so you can easily add your family's name and customize your own table of contents.

CHAPTER 15:

Your (Finally!) Organized Kitchen

. . . .

This short book on organizing your kitchen is meant to be read quickly. I hope it inspires you to jump out of your seat with a YIPEE and a desire to organize your kitchen quickly.

You now have a simple five-step system to inspire you all the way through your kitchen organizing project, including your pantry.

You have some new tools to help control paper in your kitchen. You may need to use resources in addition to this book to solve larger household paper management issues, but you can get started in the kitchen.

You now have a plan to stay organized. Once you have gone beyond sorting, you'll create organizing systems as described in this book. When you do, staying organized takes just a few minutes here and there, instead of hours and days.

You may have some non-standard kitchen spaces that have you stumped, and if that's the case, I invite you to join my free Clutter-Free Facebook Group at https://www.facebook.com/groups/heartworkorganizing/ and share your organizing challenge. It's a community of people who are trying to get organized, just like you.

Kitchen organizing isn't just one simple thing. A kitchen is the heart of the home. Kitchen organizing involves organizing stuff, making the best use out of your unique space, taking your family's preferences and tastes into account, and caring for the people (and pets) that inhabit your home.

I wrote this book with YOU in mind. I'd love to hear how it helps you.

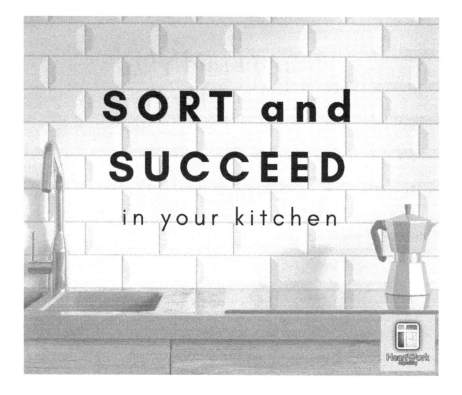

Daily Kitchen Cleaning Checklist

....

A clean kitchen is easier to keep organized, and an organized kitchen is easier to keep clean. Take ten minutes each day for these steps, and you'll have a tidy kitchen that is both clean and organized.

You don't need any special equipment for this daily routine. Just use a sponge or cloth that you already have in your sink along with warm water.

Don't let the size of this list overwhelm you. Set a timer for five or ten minutes, and move quickly until the alarm goes off to see how much you can get done. Some days you can even skip steps. Stay on top of little messes with a swipe so they don't become big messes that require scrubbing. Soon these tiny tasks will become habits.

1. Soak dried-on spots on the stove, countertops or microwave, and let them sit while you do the next tasks. Use water, water and vinegar, or water and baking soda to loosen debris.

2. Wash all dishes or put them in the dishwasher immediately for later washing.

3. Put all food back in the cabinet, pantry, refrigerator or freezer.

4. Wipe down all countertops and eating areas, like the kitchen table or bar. Save a step and use the sponge or kitchen cloth that's out right now. No need to dirty another cloth.

5. Quickly wipe down the faucet handles, spout and sink.

6. Check any fruit that might be sitting out to ripen. Eat when ripe, or put back in the refrigerator.

7. Return to the dried-on food spots soaking on the stove, countertops or microwave and wipe clean.

8. Spot sweep the floors, especially around the trash can, around pet bowls and under the cabinets, to reduce the chance of attracting ants and pests.

9. Spot clean the floors from sticky spills and drips.

10. If needed, wipe the lid to the trash bin or the handle to the trash can cabinet.

11. Toss the sponge or cloth that you've been using into the laundry. Put out fresh kitchen towels and a sponge or wash cloth each day to reduce bacteria in the kitchen.

12. Change the trash bag and take out the trash. Sprinkle baking soda to control odors in the bottom of the trash bin before putting a new trash bag inside.

For extra credit, run your dishwasher every night, even if there is some space left inside. It costs next to nothing (see chapter 13). Routinely washing at night leads to putting away clean dishes each morning, which means you'll have an empty dishwasher to start the day. Put dishes right into the dishwasher, and dishes never have a chance to stack up in the sink. It's a vicious and effective cycle, and one that leads to a cleaner kitchen that stays organized longer.

MORE FREE KITCHEN GUIDES

. . . .

Remember to request your free kitchen bonuses at Kitchen.HeartWorkOrg.com. Here's what you'll receive:

1. Report on 10 Ways to Make Your Corner Cabinets Work Better.

2. Free downloadable Family Favorites recipe binder cover, customizable table of contents and spine label. You can download a Microsoft Word version and easily customize it with your family's name.

3. Printable version of the Daily Kitchen Cleaning Checklist (from the previous section).

RECIPE FOR AN AUTHOR

· ·

Take one medium organizing nerd (Darla DeMorrow), add an MBA, a Professional Organizer® certification and a Professional Photo Organizer certification.

Steep in NAPO.net and APPO.org memberships for over a decade.

Take out of the frying pan and put directly into the fire of business ownership for HeartWork Organizing, LLC starting in 2005.

Add husband, then two kids, then French-speaking, cello-loving, poor-excuse-for-an-alarm-clock Siamese cat.

Be sure her kitchen spices are alphabetized and soup cans are on step-risers.

Season with a first book, *The Pregnant Entrepreneur*, the original book to help women handle pregnancy's emotional and financial baby bumps while running their own business.

Generously add even more of a second book, *Organizing Your Home with SORT and Succeed*, which shows you how to apply these same five steps to organizing any space in your home.

Serve with a side of more books in the SORT and Succeed series, including *Organizing Your Money with SORT and Succeed*, available in 2019.

Hungry for more? Subscribe to the blog at Https://HeartWorkOrg.com for free organizing education and inspiration.

REVIEWS ARE ICING
ON THE CAKE

....

Reviews *are very important to an author like me. If you've enjoyed this book, even if you're still working through it, could you take a minute to leave a review? Just a sentence or two about what you really liked will help other readers. Please leave a review where you bought*
Organizing Your Kitchen with SORT and Succeed.

ACKNOWLEDGEMENTS

. . . .

Thanks very much to folks who helped this book while it was baking:
Megan Wing, Nicole Gallela, Nina Amir, Robin Samrow,
HaeWon Miller and Cassandra Arnold.

REFERENCES

[i] MasterBrand Cabinets, Inc., *Can't Relax? It May Be Your Messy Kitchen. Data Reveals New Truths About Home Organization*. PRnewswire, Jun 26, 2018. https://www.prnewswire.com/news-releases/cant-relax-it-may-be-your-messy-kitchen-300672427.html

[ii] Diana Goovaerts, *More than 40 Percent of Americans Have Tech. What's Stopping the Rest?* May 19, 2017. https://www.ecnmag.com/data-focus/2017/05/more-40-percent-americans-have-adopted-smart-home-tech-whats-stopping-rest

[iii] Rob Stott, *More than Half of U.S. Homes will be Smart Homes by 2021*. July 17, 2017. https://www.dealerscope.com/article/half-u-s-homes-will-smart-homes-2021/

[iv] MasterBrand Cabinets, Inc., *Can't Relax? It May Be Your Messy Kitchen. Data Reveals New Truths About Home Organization*. PRnewswire, Jun 26, 2018. https://www.prnewswire.com/news-releases/cant-relax-it-may-be-your-messy-kitchen-300672427.html

[v] Nanci Hellmich, *9 Ways to Lose Weight by Rearranging Your Kitchen*. USA TODAY, Aug. 26, 2014. http://www.usatoday.com/story/news/nation/2014/08/26/kitchen-makeover-slim-by-design/14619799/

[vi] PECO Fridge & Freezer Recycling. https://www.peco.com/WaysToSave/ForYourHome/Pages/Recycling.aspx

[vii] Matt Hayes, *What's On Your Countertop Might Predict Your Weight*. Cornell Chronicle. October 20, 2015. 2015 Cornell study found that what's on your counter might predict your weight

[viii] Moen Clutter Zones Research Study, *CONQUER CLUTTER ZONES: Moen Uncovers Where Clutter Lives in the Home*. August 2015. http://www.moen.com/pressroom/

[ix] Kelly McGonigal, *The Willpower Instinct, How Self-Control Works, Why it Matters, and What You Can Do to Get More of It*, Avery: 1st edition, 2011.

[x] Vernon Trollinger, *How Much Electricity Does a Dishwasher Use?* March 15, 2018. https://www.bounceenergy.com/blog/2018/03/how-much-electricity-does-a-dishwasher-use/